BATTLE OF THE FLESH VS. THE SPIRIT:
A STUDY OF THE LIFE OF JACOB

Retreat/Group Companion
WORKBOOK
RICHARD T. CASE

Acknowledgments

I wish to dedicate this course to and thank all of the leaders of our **Ministry: All For Jesus—ABIDE Ministries** along with my wife. Linda, who have all walked together with us as we receive and live out the life of the Spirit, knowing we have a battle with the flesh. These leaders faithfully have consistently shared the constant struggle with this battle; and walked together into the victory of life in the Spirit in each of our personal lives. Then they all have been teaching their groups and friends how to understand this battle and walked with them to then also live out the victory of life in the Spirit. Most importantly, they all know that living in the flesh is not to be accepted as normal, but rather living in the Spirit is to be normal, and as we then do struggle with the flesh. we experience the awareness of this, now the remedy of immediate return to the Kingdom and life of God. and thus live normally in the fullness of the Spirit, as intended. This course presents such important truths and we are blessed that we all. especially Linda. have fully embraced this and are being blessed as they give it away—and literally hundreds of others are now receiving it and giving it away. Overcoming this battle is so important to the church universal—God's way of us living with Him to receive the superabundant life—Thank you all:

These leaders are:
Jake & Mary Beckel
Joe & Leigh Bogar
Rich & Janet Cocchiaro
Larry & Sherry Collet
Scott & Kristen Cornell
David & Melissa Dunkel
Tom & Susanne Ewing
Rick & Kelly Ferris
Joel & Christina Gunn
Scott & Terry Hitchcock
Rick & Nancy Hoover
Tad & Monica Jones
Ed & Becky Kobel
Don & Rachelle Light
Chris & Heidi May
Terry & Josephine Noetzel
Towanda Norton
Steve & Carolyn Van Ooteghem
Preston & Lynda Pitts
Dan & Kathy Rocconi
Bob & Keri Rockwell
John & Michelle Santaferraro
Allyson & Denny Weinberg
Neal & Kathy Weisenburger

Further, it is a joy for me to share this life with my wife. Linda. and family who together are enjoying the fruits of overcoming this battle. What an honor and a privilege for us.

BATTLE OF THE FLESH VS THE SPIRIT: A STUDY OF THE LIFE OF JACOB
COMPANION WORKBOOK
PUBLISHED BY LIVING WATERS—ABIDE MINISTRIES
7615 Lemon Gulch Way
Castle Rock, CO 80108

Unless otherwise noted, all Scripture quotations are from the ESV® Bible (The Holy Bible, English Standard Version®), copyright © 2001 by Crossway Bibles, a publishing ministry of Good News Publishers. Used by permission. All rights reserved.

ISBN: 979-8-21811534-0
Copyright © 2024 by Richard T. Case.

All rights reserved. No part of this publication may be reproduced, distributed or transmitted in any form or by any means, including photocopying, recording, or other electronic or mechanical methods, without the prior written permission of the publisher.

Publisher's Cataloging-in-Publication data

Names:
Title:
Description: .
Identifiers: ISBN | LCCN
Subjects:

Printed in the United States of America 2024 — 2nd ed

TABLE OF CONTENTS

Lesson One:
Cause of the Battle of the Flesh & Consequences; Covenant For Abraham For Believers—
Struggle of the Flesh 2

Lesson Two:
Difference Between Esau (Representing Life in the Flesh)
And Jacob (Representing Life in the Spirit) 16

Lesson Three:
Jacob's Battle of the Flesh, Experience of Victory Over the Flesh,
God's Faithfulness Despite the Flesh 28

Lesson Four:
Jacob's Wrestling With God As He Understands Surrender;
Israel's Continued Battle With the Flesh/ the Enemy (Esau's Descendants). 38

Lesson Five:
How We Life in the Spirit And Experience God's Power Over the Flesh And the Enemy 50

LESSON 1:
CAUSE OF THE BATTLE OF THE FLESH & CONSEQUENCES; COVENANT FOR ABRAHAM FOR BELIEVERS—STRUGGLE OF THE FLESH

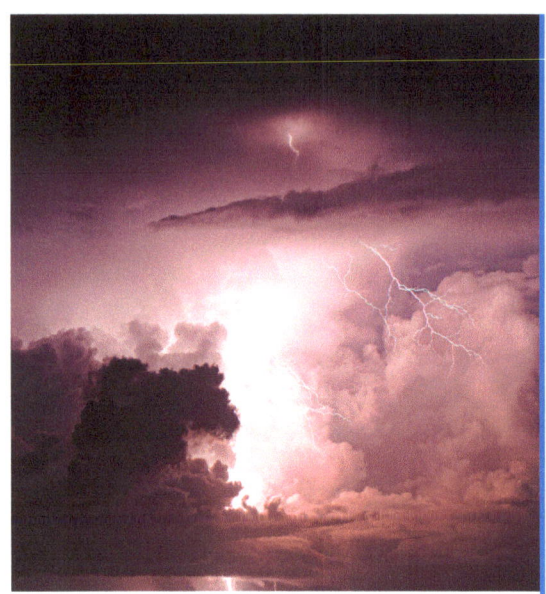

Read through these verses and write out the description of the battle of the flesh. What is the outcome of this battle for how we live out our lives? Why?

Read Romans 7:18-23: 18

18 For I know that nothing good dwells in me, that is, in my flesh. For I have the desire to do what is right, but not the ability to carry it out. 19 For I do not do the good I want, but the evil I do not want is what I keep on doing. 20 Now if I do what I do not want, it is no longer I who do it, but sin that dwells within me.

21 So I find it to be a law that when I want to do right, evil lies close at hand. 22 For I delight in the law of God, in my inner being, 23 but I see in my members another law waging war against the law of my mind and making me captive to the law of sin that dwells in my members.

> "Most believers realize they have a sinful nature, thinking "Isn't that normal, and aren't I basically going to fail even though I'm trying to be a solid Christian?"

_____
_____
_____
_____
_____
_____

LESSON 1:
CAUSE OF THE BATTLE OF THE FLESH & CONSEQUENCES; COVENANT FOR ABRAHAM FOR BELIEVERS—STRUGGLE OF THE FLESH

Read through these verses and write out what you see as both the conflict and the consequences if we continue to operate in the flesh (self).

> **Read Galatians 5:17:**
>
> [17] For the desires of the flesh are against the Spirit, and the desires of the Spirit are against the flesh, for these are opposed to each other, to keep you from doing the things you want to do.

_____
_____
_____
_____
_____

> **Read Romans 8:5–8:**
>
> [5] For those who live according to the flesh set their minds on the things of the flesh, but those who live according to the Spirit set their minds on the things of the Spirit. [6] For to set the mind on the flesh is death, but to set the mind on the Spirit is life and peace. [7] For the mind that is set on the flesh is hostile to God, for it does not submit to God's law; indeed, it cannot. [8] Those who are in the flesh cannot please God.

_____
_____
_____
_____
_____

LESSON 1:
CAUSE OF THE BATTLE OF THE FLESH & CONSEQUENCES; COVENANT FOR ABRAHAM FOR BELIEVERS—STRUGGLE OF THE FLESH

Read through these verses and write out what the Covenant is and what the primary benefits of the Covenant are to us.

THE COVENANT:

> **Read Genesis 12:1–3:**
>
> The Call of Abram
> **12** Now the Lord said[a] to Abram, "Go from your country[b] and your kindred and your father's house to the land that I will show you. ² And I will make of you a great nation, and I will bless you and make your name great, so that you will be a blessing. ³ I will bless those who bless you, and him who dishonors you I will curse, and in you all the families of the earth shall be blessed."[c]

_____
_____
_____
_____
_____

> **Read Genesis 17:1–10:**
>
> Abraham and the Covenant of Circumcision
> **17** When Abram was ninety-nine years old the Lord appeared to Abram and said to him, "I am God Almighty;[a] walk before me, and be blameless, ² that I may make my covenant between me and you, and may multiply you greatly." ³ Then Abram fell on his face. And God said to him, ⁴ "Behold, my covenant is with you, and you shall be the father of a multitude of nations. ⁵ No longer shall your name be called Abram,[b] but your name shall be Abraham,[c] for I have made you the father of a multitude of nations. ⁶ I will make you exceedingly fruitful, and I will make you into nations, and kings shall come from you. ⁷ And I will establish my covenant between me and you and your offspring after you throughout their generations for an everlasting covenant, to be God to you and to your offspring after you. ⁸ And I will give to you and to your offspring after you the land of your sojournings, all the land of Canaan, for an everlasting possession, and I will be their God."

LESSON 1:
CAUSE OF THE BATTLE OF THE FLESH & CONSEQUENCES; COVENANT FOR ABRAHAM FOR BELIEVERS—STRUGGLE OF THE FLESH

> [9] And God said to Abraham, "As for you, you shall keep my covenant, you and your offspring after you throughout their generations. [10] This is my covenant, which you shall keep, between me and you and your offspring after you: Every male among you shall be circumcised.

_____
_____
_____
_____
_____

Read through these verses and write out who the recipient of the Covenant really is. Why is that important to us as believers?

> **Read Galatians 3:15–20:**
>
> The Law and the Promise
>
> [15] To give a human example, brothers:[a] even with a man-made covenant, no one annuls it or adds to it once it has been ratified. [16] Now the promises were made to Abraham and to his offspring. It does not say, "And to offsprings," referring to many, but referring to one, "And to your offspring," who is Christ. [17] This is what I mean: the law, which came 430 years afterward, does not annul a covenant previously ratified by God, so as to make the promise void. [18] For if the inheritance comes by the law, it no longer comes by promise; but God gave it to Abraham by a promise.
>
> [19] Why then the law? It was added because of transgressions, until the offspring should come to whom the promise had been made, and it was put in place through angels by an intermediary. [20] Now an intermediary implies more than one, but God is one.

_____
_____
_____
_____
_____

LESSON 1:
CAUSE OF THE BATTLE OF THE FLESH & CONSEQUENCES; COVENANT FOR ABRAHAM FOR BELIEVERS—STRUGGLE OF THE FLESH

Read through these verses and write out what happened when Abraham and Sarah acted in the flesh (self). Why did they act this way, and what was the consequence? Why is that important to us?

> **Read Genesis 20:1–10:**
>
> Abraham and Abimelech
> **20** From there Abraham journeyed toward the territory of the Negeb and lived between Kadesh and Shur; and he sojourned in Gerar. ² And Abraham said of Sarah his wife, "She is my sister." And Abimelech king of Gerar sent and took Sarah. ³ But God came to Abimelech in a dream by night and said to him, "Behold, you are a dead man because of the woman whom you have taken, for she is a man's wife." ⁴ Now Abimelech had not approached her. So he said, "Lord, will you kill an innocent people? ⁵ Did he not himself say to me, 'She is my sister'? And she herself said, 'He is my brother.' In the integrity of my heart and the innocence of my hands I have done this." ⁶ Then God said to him in the dream, "Yes, I know that you have done this in the integrity of your heart, and it was I who kept you from sinning against me. Therefore, I did not let you touch her. ⁷ Now then, return the man's wife, for he is a prophet, so that he will pray for you, and you shall live. But if you do not return her, know that you shall surely die, you and all who are yours."
>
> ⁸ So Abimelech rose early in the morning and called all his servants and told them all these things. And the men were very much afraid. ⁹ Then Abimelech called Abraham and said to him, "What have you done to us? And how have I sinned against you, that you have brought on me and my kingdom a great sin? You have done to me things that ought not to be done." ¹⁰ And Abimelech said to Abraham, "What did you see, that you did this thing?"

_____
_____
_____
_____
_____

LESSON 1:
CAUSE OF THE BATTLE OF THE FLESH & CONSEQUENCES; COVENANT FOR ABRAHAM FOR BELIEVERS—STRUGGLE OF THE FLESH

Read through these verses and write out what we are to do regarding our flesh (self). What choice do we have, and why is this so important to choose rightly?

> **Read Galatians 4:21–31:**
>
> Example of Hagar and Sarah
> [21] Tell me, you who desire to be under the law, do you not listen to the law? [22] For it is written that Abraham had two sons, one by a slave woman and one by a free woman. [23] But the son of the slave was born according to the flesh, while the son of the free woman was born through promise. [24] Now this may be interpreted allegorically: these women are two covenants. One is from Mount Sinai, bearing children for slavery; she is Hagar. [25] Now Hagar is Mount Sinai in Arabia;[a] she corresponds to the present Jerusalem, for she is in slavery with her children. [26] But the Jerusalem above is free, and she is our mother. [27] For it is written,
>
> "Rejoice, O barren one who does not bear;
>   break forth and cry aloud, you who are not in labor!
> For the children of the desolate one will be more
>   than those of the one who has a husband."
>
> [28] Now you,[b] brothers, like Isaac, are children of promise. [29] But just as at that time he who was born according to the flesh persecuted him who was born according to the Spirit, so also it is now. [30] But what does the Scripture say? "Cast out the slave woman and her son, for the son of the slave woman shall not inherit with the son of the free woman." [31] So, brothers, we are not children of the slave but of the free woman.

_____
_____
_____
_____
_____

LESSON 1:
CAUSE OF THE BATTLE OF THE FLESH & CONSEQUENCES; COVENANT FOR ABRAHAM FOR BELIEVERS—STRUGGLE OF THE FLESH

Read through these verses and write out the choices that are set before us. What is important to choose rightly? Why is this so critical to our walk with God and experiencing the Covenant?

> **Read Deuteronomy 30:11–20:**
>
> The Choice of Life and Death
>
> [11] "For this commandment that I command you today is not too hard for you, neither is it far off. [12] It is not in heaven, that you should say, 'Who will ascend to heaven for us and bring it to us, that we may hear it and do it?' [13] Neither is it beyond the sea, that you should say, 'Who will go over the sea for us and bring it to us, that we may hear it and do it?' [14] But the word is very near you. It is in your mouth and in your heart, so that you can do it.
>
> [15] "See, I have set before you today life and good, death and evil. [16] If you obey the commandments of the Lord your God[a] that I command you today, by loving the Lord your God, by walking in his ways, and by keeping his commandments and his statutes and his rules,[b] then you shall live and multiply, and the Lord your God will bless you in the land that you are entering to take possession of it. [17] But if your heart turns away, and you will not hear, but are drawn away to worship other gods and serve them, [18] I declare to you today, that you shall surely perish. You shall not live long in the land that you are going over the Jordan to enter and possess. [19] I call heaven and earth to witness against you today, that I have set before you life and death, blessing and curse. Therefore, choose life, that you and your offspring may live, [20] loving the Lord your God, obeying his voice and holding fast to him, for he is your life and length of days, that you may dwell in the land that the Lord swore to your fathers, to Abraham, to Isaac, and to Jacob, to give them."

_____
_____
_____
_____
_____

LESSON 1:
CAUSE OF THE BATTLE OF THE FLESH & CONSEQUENCES; COVENANT FOR ABRAHAM FOR BELIEVERS—STRUGGLE OF THE FLESH

Read through these verses and write out the description of each character: Jacob and Esau. What do each represent? What strikes you about what happened as it relates to how we respond to God?

Read Genesis 25:7–28:

7 These are the days of the years of Abraham's life, 175 years. 8 Abraham breathed his last and died in a good old age, an old man and full of years, and was gathered to his people. 9 Isaac and Ishmael his sons buried him in the cave of Machpelah, in the field of Ephron the son of Zohar the Hittite, east of Mamre, 10 the field that Abraham purchased from the Hittites. There Abraham was buried, with Sarah his wife. 11 After the death of Abraham, God blessed Isaac his son. And Isaac settled at Beer-lahai-roi.

12 These are the generations of Ishmael, Abraham's son, whom Hagar the Egyptian, Sarah's servant, bore to Abraham. 13 These are the names of the sons of Ishmael, named in the order of their birth: Nebaioth, the firstborn of Ishmael; and Kedar, Adbeel, Mibsam, 14 Mishma, Dumah, Massa, 15 Hadad, Tema, Jetur, Naphish, and Kedemah. 16 These are the sons of Ishmael and these are their names, by their villages and by their encampments, twelve princes according to their tribes. 17 (These are the years of the life of Ishmael: 137 years. He breathed his last and died, and was gathered to his people.) 18 They settled from Havilah to Shur, which is opposite Egypt in the direction of Assyria. He settled[a] over against all his kinsmen.

The Birth of Esau and Jacob

19 These are the generations of Isaac, Abraham's son: Abraham fathered Isaac, 20 and Isaac was forty years old when he took Rebekah, the daughter of Bethuel the Aramean of Paddan-aram, the sister of Laban the Aramean, to be his wife. 21 And Isaac prayed to the Lord for his wife, because she was barren. And the Lord granted his prayer, and Rebekah his wife conceived. 22 The children struggled together within her, and she said, "If it is thus, why is this happening to me?"[b] So she went to inquire of the Lord. 23 And the Lord said to her,

"Two nations are in your womb,
    and two peoples from within you[c] shall be divided;
the one shall be stronger than the other,
    the older shall serve the younger."

LESSON 1:
CAUSE OF THE BATTLE OF THE FLESH & CONSEQUENCES; COVENANT FOR ABRAHAM FOR BELIEVERS—STRUGGLE OF THE FLESH

> [24] When her days to give birth were completed, behold, there were twins in her womb. [25] The first came out red, all his body like a hairy cloak, so they called his name Esau. [26] Afterward his brother came out with his hand holding Esau's heel, so his name was called Jacob.[d] Isaac was sixty years old when she bore them.
>
> [27] When the boys grew up, Esau was a skillful hunter, a man of the field, while Jacob was a quiet man, dwelling in tents. [28] Isaac loved Esau because he ate of his game, but Rebekah loved Jacob.

_____
_____
_____
_____
_____

> **Read Genesis 25:29–34:**
>
> Esau Sells His Birthright
> [29] Once when Jacob was cooking stew, Esau came in from the field, and he was exhausted. [30] And Esau said to Jacob, "Let me eat some of that red stew, for I am exhausted!" (Therefore his name was called Edom.[a]) [31] Jacob said, "Sell me your birthright now." [32] Esau said, "I am about to die; of what use is a birthright to me?" [33] Jacob said, "Swear to me now." So he swore to him and sold his birthright to Jacob. [34] Then Jacob gave Esau bread and lentil stew, and he ate and drank and rose and went his way. Thus Esau despised his birthright.

_____
_____
_____
_____
_____

LESSON 1:
CAUSE OF THE BATTLE OF THE FLESH & CONSEQUENCES; COVENANT FOR ABRAHAM FOR BELIEVERS—STRUGGLE OF THE FLESH

> **Read again Genesis 25:34:**
>
> [34] Then Jacob gave Esau bread and lentil stew, and he ate and drank and rose and went his way. Thus, Esau despised his birthright.

_____
_____
_____
_____
_____

Read through these verses and write out the reason God hated Esau. Since this seems rather harsh and against God's nature, how might we explain this, and what is the significance to us?

> **Read Malachi 1:1–5:**
>
> **1** The oracle of the word of the Lord to Israel by Malachi.[a]
>
> The Lord's Love for Israel
>
> [2] "I have loved you," says the Lord. But you say, "How have you loved us?" "Is not Esau Jacob's brother?" declares the Lord. "Yet I have loved Jacob [3] but Esau I have hated. I have laid waste his hill country and left his heritage to jackals of the desert." [4] If Edom says, "We are shattered but we will rebuild the ruins," the Lord of hosts says, "They may build, but I will tear down, and they will be called 'the wicked country,' and 'the people with whom the Lord is angry forever.'" [5] Your own eyes shall see this, and you shall say, "Great is the Lord beyond the border of Israel!"

_____
_____
_____
_____
_____

LESSON 1:
CAUSE OF THE BATTLE OF THE FLESH & CONSEQUENCES; COVENANT FOR ABRAHAM FOR BELIEVERS—STRUGGLE OF THE FLESH

Read through these verses and write out what the difference is between living in the Spirit and living in the flesh. How might we interpret this for our lives today? Why?

> **Read Obadiah 1:1–16:**
>
> [1] The vision of Obadiah.
>
> Edom Will Be Humbled
>
> Thus says the Lord God concerning Edom:
> We have heard a report from the Lord,
>   and a messenger has been sent among the nations:
> "Rise up! Let us rise against her for battle!"
> [2] Behold, I will make you small among the nations;
>   you shall be utterly despised.[a]
> [3] The pride of your heart has deceived you,
>   you who live in the clefts of the rock,[b]
>   in your lofty dwelling,
> who say in your heart,
>   "Who will bring me down to the ground?"
> [4] Though you soar aloft like the eagle,
>   though your nest is set among the stars,
>   from there I will bring you down,
> declares the Lord.
> [5] If thieves came to you,
>   if plunderers came by night—
>   how you have been destroyed!—
>   would they not steal only enough for themselves?
> If grape gatherers came to you,
>   would they not leave gleanings?
> [6] How Esau has been pillaged,
>   his treasures sought out!
> [7] All your allies have driven you to your border;
>   those at peace with you have deceived you;
> they have prevailed against you;
>   those who eat your bread[c] have set a trap beneath you—
>   you have[d] no understanding.

LESSON 1:
CAUSE OF THE BATTLE OF THE FLESH & CONSEQUENCES; COVENANT FOR ABRAHAM FOR BELIEVERS—STRUGGLE OF THE FLESH

[8] Will I not on that day, declares the Lord,
　　destroy the wise men out of Edom,
　　and understanding out of Mount Esau?
[9] And your mighty men shall be dismayed, O Teman,
　　so that every man from Mount Esau will be cut off by slaughter.

Edom's Violence Against Jacob

[10] Because of the violence done to your brother Jacob,
　　shame shall cover you,
　　and you shall be cut off forever.
[11] On the day that you stood aloof,
　　on the day that strangers carried off his wealth
and foreigners entered his gates
　　and cast lots for Jerusalem,
　　you were like one of them.
[12] But do not gloat over the day of your brother
　　in the day of his misfortune;
do not rejoice over the people of Judah
　　in the day of their ruin;
do not boast[e]
　　in the day of distress.
[13] Do not enter the gate of my people
　　in the day of their calamity;
do not gloat over his disaster
　　in the day of his calamity;
do not loot his wealth
　　in the day of his calamity.
[14] Do not stand at the crossroads
　　to cut off his fugitives;
do not hand over his survivors
　　in the day of distress.

The Day of the Lord Is Near

[15] For the day of the Lord is near upon all the nations.
As you have done, it shall be done to you;
　　your deeds shall return on your own head.
[16] For as you have drunk on my holy mountain,
　　so all the nations shall drink continually;
they shall drink and swallow,
　　and shall be as though they had never been.

LESSON 1:
CAUSE OF THE BATTLE OF THE FLESH & CONSEQUENCES; COVENANT FOR ABRAHAM FOR BELIEVERS—STRUGGLE OF THE FLESH

_____
_____
_____
_____
_____

Read through these verses and write out why God did not accept Esau's supposed repentance. How might we understand this for our lives today?

> **Read Hebrews 12:12–17:**
>
> [12] Therefore lift your drooping hands and strengthen your weak knees, [13] and make straight paths for your feet, so that what is lame may not be put out of joint but rather be healed. [14] Strive for peace with everyone, and for the holiness without which no one will see the Lord. [15] See to it that no one fails to obtain the grace of God; that no "root of bitterness" springs up and causes trouble, and by it many become defiled; [16] that no one is sexually immoral or unholy like Esau, who sold his birthright for a single meal. [17] For you know that afterward, when he desired to inherit the blessing, he was rejected, for he found no chance to repent, though he sought it with tears.

_____
_____
_____
_____
_____

LESSON 2:
DIFFERENCE BETWEEN ESAU (REPRESENTING LIFE IN THE FLESH) AND JACOB (REPRESENTING LIFE IN THE SPIRIT)

"As believers, we must be in Christ and choose to live in the Spirit and receive the Covenant."

Read through these verses and write out why God continually had Isaac move from place to place. What do you understand about the wiles, strategies, and tactics of the enemy? How does this affect us?

Read Genesis 26:1–35:

God's Promise to Isaac
26 Now there was a famine in the land, besides the former famine that was in the days of Abraham. And Isaac went to Gerar to Abimelech king of the Philistines. [2] And the Lord appeared to him and said, "Do not go down to Egypt; dwell in the land of which I shall tell you. [3] Sojourn in this land, and I will be with you and will bless you, for to you and to your offspring I will give all these lands, and I will establish the oath that I swore to Abraham your father. [4] I will multiply your offspring as the stars of heaven and will give to your offspring all these lands. And in your offspring all the nations of the earth shall be blessed, [5] because Abraham obeyed my voice and kept my charge, my commandments, my statutes, and my laws."

Isaac and Abimelech
[6] So Isaac settled in Gerar. [7] When the men of the place asked him about his wife, he said, "She is my sister," for he feared to say, "My wife," thinking, "lest the men of the place should kill me because of Rebekah," because she was attractive in appearance. [8] When he had been there a long time, Abimelech, king of the Philistines looked out of a window and saw Isaac laughing with[a] Rebekah his wife. [9] So Abimelech called Isaac and said, "Behold, she is your wife. How then could you say, 'She is my sister'?" Isaac said to him, "Because I thought, 'Lest I die because of her.'" [10] Abimelech said, "What is this you have done to us? One of the people might easily have lain with your wife, and you would have brought guilt upon us." [11] So Abimelech warned all the people, saying, "Whoever touches this man or his wife shall surely be put to death."

LESSON 2:
DIFFERENCE BETWEEN ESAU (REPRESENTING LIFE IN THE FLESH) AND JACOB (REPRESENTING LIFE IN THE SPIRIT)

[12] And Isaac sowed in that land and reaped in the same year a hundredfold. The Lord blessed him, [13] and the man became rich, and gained more and more until he became very wealthy. [14] He had possessions of flocks and herds and many servants, so that the Philistines envied him. [15] (Now the Philistines had stopped and filled with earth all the wells that his father's servants had dug in the days of Abraham his father.) [16] And Abimelech said to Isaac, "Go away from us, for you are much mightier than we."

[17] So Isaac departed from there and encamped in the Valley of Gerar and settled there. [18] And Isaac dug again the wells of water that had been dug in the days of Abraham his father, which the Philistines had stopped after the death of Abraham. And he gave them the names that his father had given them. [19] But when Isaac's servants dug in the valley and found there a well of spring water, [20] the herdsmen of Gerar quarreled with Isaac's herdsmen, saying, "The water is ours." So he called the name of the well Esek,[b] because they contended with him. [21] Then they dug another well, and they quarreled over that also, so he called its name Sitnah.[c] [22] And he moved from there and dug another well, and they did not quarrel over it. So he called its name Rehoboth,[d] saying, "For now the Lord has made room for us, and we shall be fruitful in the land."

[23] From there he went up to Beersheba. [24] And the Lord appeared to him the same night and said, "I am the God of Abraham your father. Fear not, for I am with you and will bless you and multiply your offspring for my servant Abraham's sake." [25] So he built an altar there and called upon the name of the Lord and pitched his tent there. And there Isaac's servants dug a well. [26] When Abimelech went to him from Gerar with Ahuzzath his adviser and Phicol the commander of his army, [27] Isaac said to them, "Why have you come to me, seeing that you hate me and have sent me away from you?" [28] They said, "We see plainly that the Lord has been with you. So we said, let there be a sworn pact between us, between you and us, and let us make a Covenant with you, [29] that you will do us no harm, just as we have not touched you and have done to you nothing but good and have sent you away in peace. You are now the blessed of the Lord." [30] So he made them a feast, and they ate and drank. [31] In the morning they rose early and exchanged oaths. And Isaac sent them on their way, and they departed from him in peace. [32] That same day Isaac's servants came and told him about the well that they had dug and said to him, "We have found water." [33] He called it Shibah;[e] therefore the name of the city is Beersheba to this day.

LESSON 2:
DIFFERENCE BETWEEN ESAU (REPRESENTING LIFE IN THE FLESH) AND JACOB (REPRESENTING LIFE IN THE SPIRIT)

> ³⁴ When Esau was forty years old, he took Judith the daughter of Beeri the Hittite to be his wife, and Basemath the daughter of Elon the Hittite, ³⁵ and they made life bitter[f] for Isaac and Rebekah.

_____

_____

_____

_____

_____

Read through these verses and write out how Jacob and Rebecca deceived Isaac. With this deception, how could Jacob actually be the recipient of the blessing? What does this mean for us?

> **Read Genesis 27:1–40:**
>
> Isaac Blesses Jacob
> **27** When Isaac was old and his eyes were dim so that he could not see, he called Esau his older son and said to him, "My son"; and he answered, "Here I am." ² He said, "Behold, I am old; I do not know the day of my death. ³ Now then, take your weapons, your quiver and your bow, and go out to the field and hunt game for me, ⁴ and prepare for me delicious food, such as I love, and bring it to me so that I may eat, that my soul may bless you before I die."
>
> ⁵ Now Rebekah was listening when Isaac spoke to his son Esau. So when Esau went to the field to hunt for game and bring it, ⁶ Rebekah said to her son Jacob, "I heard your father speak to your brother Esau, ⁷ 'Bring me game and prepare for me delicious food, that I may eat it and bless you before the Lord before I die.' ⁸ Now therefore, my son, obey my voice as I command you. ⁹ Go to the flock and bring me two good young goats, so that I may prepare from them delicious food for your father, such as he loves. ¹⁰ And you shall bring it to your father to eat, so that he may bless you before he dies." ¹¹ But Jacob said to Rebekah his mother, "Behold, my brother Esau is a hairy man, and I am a smooth man. ¹² Perhaps my father will feel me, and I shall seem to be mocking him and bring a curse upon myself and not a blessing." ¹³ His mother said to him, "Let your curse be on me, my son; only obey my voice, and go, bring them to me." ¹⁴ So he went and took them and brought them to his mother, and his mother

LESSON 2:
DIFFERENCE BETWEEN ESAU (REPRESENTING LIFE IN THE FLESH) AND JACOB (REPRESENTING LIFE IN THE SPIRIT)

prepared delicious food, such as his father loved. ¹⁵ Then Rebekah took the best garments of Esau her older son, which were with her in the house, and put them on Jacob her younger son. ¹⁶ And the skins of the young goats she put on his hands and on the smooth part of his neck. ¹⁷ And she put the delicious food and the bread, which she had prepared, into the hand of her son Jacob.

¹⁸ So he went in to his father and said, "My father." And he said, "Here I am. Who are you, my son?" ¹⁹ Jacob said to his father, "I am Esau your firstborn. I have done as you told me; now sit up and eat of my game, that your soul may bless me." ²⁰ But Isaac said to his son, "How is it that you have found it so quickly, my son?" He answered, "Because the Lord your God granted me success." ²¹ Then Isaac said to Jacob, "Please come near, that I may feel you, my son, to know whether you are really my son Esau or not." ²² So Jacob went near to Isaac his father, who felt him and said, "The voice is Jacob's voice, but the hands are the hands of Esau." ²³ And he did not recognize him, because his hands were hairy like his brother Esau's hands. So he blessed him. ²⁴ He said, "Are you really my son Esau?" He answered, "I am." ²⁵ Then he said, "Bring it near to me, that I may eat of my son's game and bless you." So he brought it near to him, and he ate; and he brought him wine, and he drank.

²⁶ Then his father Isaac said to him, "Come near and kiss me, my son." ²⁷ So he came near and kissed him. And Isaac smelled the smell of his garments and blessed him and said,

"See, the smell of my son
 is as the smell of a field that the Lord has blessed!
²⁸ May God give you of the dew of heaven
 and of the fatness of the earth
 and plenty of grain and wine.
²⁹ Let peoples serve you,
 and nations bow down to you.
Be lord over your brothers,
 and may your mother's sons bow down to you.
Cursed be everyone who curses you,
 and blessed be everyone who blesses you!"

³⁰ As soon as Isaac had finished blessing Jacob, when Jacob had scarcely gone out from the presence of Isaac his father, Esau his brother came in from his hunting. ³¹ He also prepared delicious food and brought it to his father. And he said to his father, "Let my father arise and eat of his son's game, that you may bless me." ³² His father Isaac said to him, "Who are you?" He answered, "I am your

LESSON 2:
DIFFERENCE BETWEEN ESAU (REPRESENTING LIFE IN THE FLESH) AND JACOB (REPRESENTING LIFE IN THE SPIRIT)

son, your firstborn, Esau." 33 Then Isaac trembled very violently and said, "Who was it then that hunted game and brought it to me, and I ate it all before you came, and I have blessed him? Yes, and he shall be blessed." 34 As soon as Esau heard the words of his father, he cried out with an exceedingly great and bitter cry and said to his father, "Bless me, even me also, O my father!" 35 But he said, "Your brother came deceitfully, and he has taken away your blessing." 36 Esau said, "Is he not rightly named Jacob?[a] For he has cheated me these two times. He took away my birthright, and behold, now he has taken away my blessing." Then he said, "Have you not reserved a blessing for me?" 37 Isaac answered and said to Esau, "Behold, I have made him lord over you, and all his brothers I have given to him for servants, and with grain and wine I have sustained him. What then can I do for you, my son?" 38 Esau said to his father, "Have you but one blessing, my father? Bless me, even me also, O my father." And Esau lifted up his voice and wept.

39 Then Isaac his father answered and said to him:
"Behold, away from[b] the fatness of the earth shall your dwelling be,
    and away from[c] the dew of heaven on high.
40 By your sword you shall live,
    and you shall serve your brother;
but when you grow restless
    you shall break his yoke from your neck."

_____
_____
_____
_____
_____

Read through these two sets of verses and write out the difference between receiving God's blessing and not receiving God's blessings. Why is this important for us?

Read Deuteronomy 28:1–14:

Blessings for Obedience
28 "And if you faithfully obey the voice of the Lord your God, being careful to do all his commandments that I command you today, the Lord your God

LESSON 2:
DIFFERENCE BETWEEN ESAU (REPRESENTING LIFE IN THE FLESH) AND JACOB (REPRESENTING LIFE IN THE SPIRIT)

> will set you high above all the nations of the earth. 2 And all these blessings shall come upon you and overtake you, if you obey the voice of the Lord your God. 3 Blessed shall you be in the city, and blessed shall you be in the field. 4 Blessed shall be the fruit of your womb and the fruit of your ground and the fruit of your cattle, the increase of your herds and the young of your flock. 5 Blessed shall be your basket and your kneading bowl. 6 Blessed shall you be when you come in, and blessed shall you be when you go out.
>
> 7 "The Lord will cause your enemies who rise against you to be defeated before you. They shall come out against you one way and flee before you seven ways. 8 The Lord will command the blessing on you in your barns and in all that you undertake. And he will bless you in the land that the Lord your God is giving you. 9 The Lord will establish you as a people holy to himself, as he has sworn to you, if you keep the commandments of the Lord your God and walk in his ways. 10 And all the peoples of the earth shall see that you are called by the name of the Lord, and they shall be afraid of you. 11 And the Lord will make you abound in prosperity, in the fruit of your womb and in the fruit of your livestock and in the fruit of your ground, within the land that the Lord swore to your fathers to give you. 12 The Lord will open to you his good treasury, the heavens, to give the rain to your land in its season and to bless all the work of your hands. And you shall lend to many nations, but you shall not borrow. 13 And the Lord will make you the head and not the tail, and you shall only go up and not down, if you obey the commandments of the Lord your God, which I command you today, being careful to do them, 14 and if you do not turn aside from any of the words that I command you today, to the right hand or to the left, to go after other gods to serve them.

_____
_____
_____
_____
_____

LESSON 2:
DIFFERENCE BETWEEN ESAU (REPRESENTING LIFE IN THE FLESH) AND JACOB (REPRESENTING LIFE IN THE SPIRIT)

Read Deuteronomy 28:15:

Curses for Disobedience
15 "But if you will not obey the voice of the Lord your God or be careful to do all his commandments and his statutes that I command you today, then all these curses shall come upon you and overtake you.

_____
_____
_____
_____
_____

Read through these verses and write out the difference between Esau and Jacob. How does this apply to our lives?

Read Genesis 28:1–9:

Jacob Sent to Laban
28 Then Isaac called Jacob and blessed him and directed him, "You must not take a wife from the Canaanite women. 2 Arise, go to Paddan-aram to the house of Bethuel your mother's father, and take as your wife from there one of the daughters of Laban your mother's brother. 3 God Almighty[a] bless you and make you fruitful and multiply you, that you may become a company of peoples. 4 May he give the blessing of Abraham to you and to your offspring with you, that you may take possession of the land of your sojournings that God gave to Abraham!" 5 Thus Isaac sent Jacob away. And he went to Paddan-aram, to Laban, the son of Bethuel the Aramean, the brother of Rebekah, Jacob's and Esau's mother.

Esau Marries an Ishmaelite
6 Now Esau saw that Isaac had blessed Jacob and sent him away to Paddan-aram to take a wife from there, and that as he blessed him he directed him, "You must not take a wife from the Canaanite women," 7 and that Jacob had obeyed his father and his mother and gone to Paddan-aram. 8 So when Esau saw that the Canaanite women did not please Isaac his father, 9 Esau went to Ishmael and took as his wife, besides the wives he had, Mahalath the daughter of Ishmael, Abraham's son, the sister of Nebaioth.

LESSON 2:
DIFFERENCE BETWEEN ESAU (REPRESENTING LIFE IN THE FLESH) AND JACOB (REPRESENTING LIFE IN THE SPIRIT)

_____
_____
_____
_____
_____

Read through these sets of verses and write out the meaning of Jacob's dream. Why is this so important to highlight in scripture, both in the Old Testament and the New Testament? And why is this significant to us?

Read Genesis 28:10–22:

Jacob's Dream

[10] Jacob left Beersheba and went toward Haran. [11] And he came to a certain place and stayed there that night, because the sun had set. Taking one of the stones of the place, he put it under his head and lay down in that place to sleep. [12] And he dreamed, and behold, there was a ladder[a] set up on the earth, and the top of it reached to heaven. And behold, the angels of God were ascending and descending on it! [13] And behold, the Lord stood above it[b] and said, "I am the Lord, the God of Abraham your father and the God of Isaac. The land on which you lie I will give to you and to your offspring. [14] Your offspring shall be like the dust of the earth, and you shall spread abroad to the west and to the east and to the north and to the south, and in you and your offspring shall all the families of the earth be blessed. [15] Behold, I am with you and will keep you wherever you go, and will bring you back to this land. For I will not leave you until I have done what I have promised you." [16] Then Jacob awoke from his sleep and said, "Surely the Lord is in this place, and I did not know it." [17] And he was afraid and said, "How awesome is this place! This is none other than the house of God, and this is the gate of heaven."

[18] So early in the morning Jacob took the stone that he had put under his head and set it up for a pillar and poured oil on the top of it. [19] He called the name of that place Bethel,[c] but the name of the city was Luz at the first. [20] Then Jacob made a vow, saying, "If God will be with me and will keep me in this way that I go, and will give me bread to eat and clothing to wear, [21] so that I come again to my father's house in peace, then the Lord shall be my God, [22] and this stone, which I have set up for a pillar, shall be God's house. And of all that you give me I will give a full tenth to you."

LESSON 2:
DIFFERENCE BETWEEN ESAU (REPRESENTING LIFE IN THE FLESH) AND JACOB (REPRESENTING LIFE IN THE SPIRIT)

_____
_____
_____
_____
_____

Read John 1:29–51:

Behold, the Lamb of God

29 The next day he saw Jesus coming toward him, and said, "Behold, the Lamb of God, who takes away the sin of the world! 30 This is he of whom I said, 'After me comes a man who ranks before me, because he was before me.' 31 I myself did not know him, but for this purpose I came baptizing with water, that he might be revealed to Israel." 32 And John bore witness: "I saw the Spirit descend from heaven like a dove, and it remained on him. 33 I myself did not know him, but he who sent me to baptize with water said to me, 'He on whom you see the Spirit descend and remain, this is he who baptizes with the Holy Spirit.' 34 And I have seen and have borne witness that this is the Son[a] of God."

Jesus Calls the First Disciples

35 The next day again John was standing with two of his disciples, 36 and he looked at Jesus as he walked by and said, "Behold, the Lamb of God!" 37 The two disciples heard him say this, and they followed Jesus. 38 Jesus turned and saw them following and said to them, "What are you seeking?" And they said to him, "Rabbi" (which means Teacher), "where are you staying?" 39 He said to them, "Come and you will see." So they came and saw where he was staying, and they stayed with him that day, for it was about the tenth hour.[b] 40 One of the two who heard John speak and followed Jesus[c] was Andrew, Simon Peter's brother. 41 He first found his own brother Simon and said to him, "We have found the Messiah" (which means Christ). 42 He brought him to Jesus. Jesus looked at him and said, "You are Simon the son of John. You shall be called Cephas" (which means Peter[d]).

Jesus Calls Philip and Nathanael

43 The next day Jesus decided to go to Galilee. He found Philip and said to him, "Follow me." 44 Now Philip was from Bethsaida, the city of Andrew and Peter. 45 Philip found Nathanael and said to him, "We have found him of whom Moses in the Law and also the prophets wrote, Jesus of Nazareth, the son of Joseph." 46 Nathanael said to him, "Can anything good come out

LESSON 2:
DIFFERENCE BETWEEN ESAU (REPRESENTING LIFE IN THE FLESH) AND JACOB (REPRESENTING LIFE IN THE SPIRIT)

> of Nazareth?" Philip said to him, "Come and see." 47 Jesus saw Nathanael coming toward him and said of him, "Behold, an Israelite indeed, in whom there is no deceit!" 48 Nathanael said to him, "How do you know me?" Jesus answered him, "Before Philip called you, when you were under the fig tree, I saw you." 49 Nathanael answered him, "Rabbi, you are the Son of God! You are the King of Israel!" 50 Jesus answered him, "Because I said to you, 'I saw you under the fig tree,' do you believe? You will see greater things than these." 51 And he said to him, "Truly, truly, I say to you,[e] you will see heaven opened, and the angels of God ascending and descending on the Son of Man."

_____
_____
_____
_____
_____

> **Read Hebrews 1:5–2:4:**
>
> 5 For to which of the angels did God ever say,
> "You are my Son,
>   today I have begotten you"?
>
> Or again,
> "I will be to him a father,
>   and he shall be to me a son"?
>
> 6 And again, when he brings the firstborn into the world, he says,
> "Let all God's angels worship him."
>
> 7 Of the angels he says,
> "He makes his angels winds,
>   and his ministers a flame of fire."
>
> 8 But of the Son he says,
> "Your throne, O God, is forever and ever,
>   the scepter of uprightness is the scepter of your kingdom.
> 9 You have loved righteousness and hated wickedness;

LESSON 2:
DIFFERENCE BETWEEN ESAU (REPRESENTING LIFE IN THE FLESH) AND JACOB (REPRESENTING LIFE IN THE SPIRIT)

therefore God, your God, has anointed you
  with the oil of gladness beyond your companions."

[10] And,
"You, Lord, laid the foundation of the earth in the beginning,
  and the heavens are the work of your hands;
[11] they will perish, but you remain;
  they will all wear out like a garment,
[12] like a robe you will roll them up,
  like a garment they will be changed.[a]
But you are the same,
  and your years will have no end."

[13] And to which of the angels has he ever said,
"Sit at my right hand
  until I make your enemies a footstool for your feet"?

[14] Are they not all ministering spirits sent out to serve for the sake of those who are to inherit salvation?

Warning Against Neglecting Salvation
2 Therefore we must pay much closer attention to what we have heard, lest we drift away from it. [2] For since the message declared by angels proved to be reliable, and every transgression or disobedience received a just retribution, [3] how shall we escape if we neglect such a great salvation? It was declared at first by the Lord, and it was attested to us by those who heard, [4] while God also bore witness by signs and wonders and various miracles and by gifts of the Holy Spirit distributed according to his will.

LESSON 3:
JACOB'S BATTLE OF THE FLESH, EXPERIENCE OF VICTORY OVER THE FLESH, GOD'S FAITHFULNESS DESPITE THE FLESH

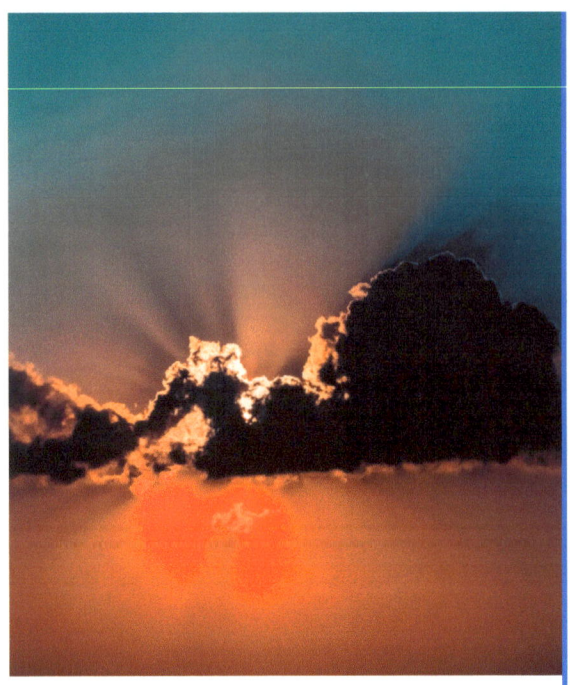

Read through these sets of verses and write out the role of the flesh in the life of Jacob. What caused this, and what were the consequences of this? Why did Jacob continue to honor his commitments even though deceit was involved? Why is that significant to us? What are the benefits of operating with integrity, and how are we to carry this out?

> **Read Genesis 29:1–30:**
>
> Jacob Marries Leah and Rachel
> **29** Then Jacob went on his journey and came to the land of the people of the east. ² As he looked, he saw a well in the field, and behold, three flocks of sheep lying beside it, for out of that well the flocks were watered. The stone on the well's mouth was large, ³ and when all the flocks were gathered there, the shepherds would roll the stone from the mouth of the well and water the sheep, and put the stone back in its place over the mouth of the well.
>
> ⁴ Jacob said to them, "My brothers, where do you come from?" They said, "We are from Haran." ⁵ He said to them, "Do you know Laban the son of Nahor?" They said, "We know him." ⁶ He said to them, "Is it well with him?" They said, "It is well; and see, Rachel his daughter is coming with the sheep!" ⁷ He said, "Behold, it is still high day; it is not time for the livestock to be gathered together. Water the sheep and go, pasture them." ⁸ But they said, "We cannot until all the flocks are gathered together and the stone is rolled from the mouth of the well; then we water the sheep."
>
> ⁹ While he was still speaking with them, Rachel came with her father's sheep, for she was a shepherdess. ¹⁰ Now as soon as Jacob saw Rachel the daughter of Laban his mother's brother, and the sheep of Laban his mother's brother, Jacob came near and rolled the stone from the well's mouth and watered the flock of Laban his mother's brother. ¹¹ Then Jacob kissed Rachel and wept aloud. ¹² And Jacob told Rachel that he was her father's kinsman, and that he was Rebekah's son, and she ran and told her father.

> **"...he invites us to live in the Spirit where the beautiful life is that God wants to deliver to us."**

LESSON 3:
JACOB'S BATTLE OF THE FLESH, EXPERIENCE OF VICTORY OVER THE FLESH, GOD'S FAITHFULNESS DESPITE THE FLESH

13 As soon as Laban heard the news about Jacob, his sister's son, he ran to meet him and embraced him and kissed him and brought him to his house. Jacob told Laban all these things, 14 and Laban said to him, "Surely you are my bone and my flesh!" And he stayed with him a month.

15 Then Laban said to Jacob, "Because you are my kinsman, should you therefore serve me for nothing? Tell me, what shall your wages be?" 16 Now Laban had two daughters. The name of the older was Leah, and the name of the younger was Rachel. 17 Leah's eyes were weak,[a] but Rachel was beautiful in form and appearance. 18 Jacob loved Rachel. And he said, "I will serve you seven years for your younger daughter Rachel." 19 Laban said, "It is better that I give her to you than that I should give her to any other man; stay with me." 20 So Jacob served seven years for Rachel, and they seemed to him but a few days because of the love he had for her.

21 Then Jacob said to Laban, "Give me my wife that I may go in to her, for my time is completed." 22 So Laban gathered together all the people of the place and made a feast. 23 But in the evening he took his daughter Leah and brought her to Jacob, and he went in to her. 24 (Laban gave[b] his female servant Zilpah to his daughter Leah to be her servant.) 25 And in the morning, behold, it was Leah! And Jacob said to Laban, "What is this you have done to me? Did I not serve with you for Rachel? Why then have you deceived me?" 26 Laban said, "It is not so done in our country, to give the younger before the firstborn. 27 Complete the week of this one, and we will give you the other also in return for serving me another seven years." 28 Jacob did so, and completed her week. Then Laban gave him his daughter Rachel to be his wife. 29 (Laban gave his female servant Bilhah to his daughter Rachel to be her servant.) 30 So Jacob went in to Rachel also, and he loved Rachel more than Leah, and served Laban for another seven years.

_____
_____
_____
_____
_____

LESSON 3:
JACOB'S BATTLE OF THE FLESH, EXPERIENCE OF VICTORY OVER THE FLESH, GOD'S FAITHFULNESS DESPITE THE FLESH

> **Read 1 Kings 9:1–9:**
>
> The Lord Appears to Solomon
>
> **9** As soon as Solomon had finished building the house of the Lord and the king's house and all that Solomon desired to build, ² the Lord appeared to Solomon a second time, as he had appeared to him at Gibeon. ³ And the Lord said to him, "I have heard your prayer and your plea, which you have made before me. I have consecrated this house that you have built, by putting my name there forever. My eyes and my heart will be there for all time. ⁴ And as for you, if you will walk before me, as David your father walked, with integrity of heart and uprightness, doing according to all that I have commanded you, and keeping my statutes and my rules, ⁵ then I will establish your royal throne over Israel forever, as I promised David your father, saying, 'You shall not lack a man on the throne of Israel.' ⁶ But if you turn aside from following me, you or your children, and do not keep my commandments and my statutes that I have set before you, but go and serve other gods and worship them, ⁷ then I will cut off Israel from the land that I have given them, and the house that I have consecrated for my name I will cast out of my sight, and Israel will become a proverb and a byword among all peoples. ⁸ And this house will become a heap of ruins.[a] Everyone passing by it will be astonished and will hiss, and they will say, 'Why has the Lord done thus to this land and to this house?' ⁹ Then they will say, 'Because they abandoned the Lord their God who brought their fathers out of the land of Egypt and laid hold on other gods and worshiped them and served them. Therefore, the Lord has brought all this disaster on them.'"

_____
_____
_____
_____
_____

LESSON 3:
JACOB'S BATTLE OF THE FLESH, EXPERIENCE OF VICTORY OVER THE FLESH, GOD'S FAITHFULNESS DESPITE THE FLESH

> **Read Proverbs 10:9–11:**
>
> [9] Whoever walks in integrity walks securely,
>   but he who makes his ways crooked will be found out.
> [10] Whoever winks the eye causes trouble,
>   and a babbling fool will come to ruin.
> [11] The mouth of the righteous is a fountain of life,
>   but the mouth of the wicked conceals violence.

_____
_____
_____
_____

> **Read Matthew 5:33–37:**
>
> Oaths
>
> [33] "Again you have heard that it was said to those of old, 'You shall not swear falsely, but shall perform to the Lord what you have sworn.' [34] But I say to you, Do not take an oath at all, either by heaven, for it is the throne of God, [35] or by the earth, for it is his footstool, or by Jerusalem, for it is the city of the great King. [36] And do not take an oath by your head, for you cannot make one hair white or black. [37] Let what you say be simply 'Yes' or 'No'; anything more than this comes from evil.[a]

_____
_____
_____
_____
_____

LESSON 3:
JACOB'S BATTLE OF THE FLESH, EXPERIENCE OF VICTORY OVER THE FLESH, GOD'S FAITHFULNESS DESPITE THE FLESH

Read Genesis 29:31–30:24:

Jacob's Children

31 When the Lord saw that Leah was hated, he opened her womb, but Rachel was barren. 32 And Leah conceived and bore a son, and she called his name Reuben,[a] for she said, "Because the Lord has looked upon my affliction; for now my husband will love me." 33 She conceived again and bore a son, and said, "Because the Lord has heard that I am hated, he has given me this son also." And she called his name Simeon.[b] 34 Again she conceived and bore a son, and said, "Now this time my husband will be attached to me, because I have borne him three sons." Therefore his name was called Levi.[c] 35 And she conceived again and bore a son, and said, "This time I will praise the Lord." Therefore she called his name Judah.[d] Then she ceased bearing.

30 When Rachel saw that she bore Jacob no children, she envied her sister. She said to Jacob, "Give me children, or I shall die!" 2 Jacob's anger was kindled against Rachel, and he said, "Am I in the place of God, who has withheld from you the fruit of the womb?" 3 Then she said, "Here is my servant Bilhah; go in to her, so that she may give birth on my behalf,[e] that even I may have children[f] through her." 4 So she gave him her servant Bilhah as a wife, and Jacob went in to her. 5 And Bilhah conceived and bore Jacob a son. 6 Then Rachel said, "God has judged me, and has also heard my voice and given me a son." Therefore she called his name Dan.[g] 7 Rachel's servant Bilhah conceived again and bore Jacob a second son. 8 Then Rachel said, "With mighty wrestlings[h] I have wrestled with my sister and have prevailed." So she called his name Naphtali.[i]

9 When Leah saw that she had ceased bearing children, she took her servant Zilpah and gave her to Jacob as a wife. 10 Then Leah's servant Zilpah bore Jacob a son. 11 And Leah said, "Good fortune has come!" so she called his name Gad.[j] 12 Leah's servant Zilpah bore Jacob a second son. 13 And Leah said, "Happy am I! For women have called me happy." So she called his name Asher.[k]

14 In the days of wheat harvest Reuben went and found mandrakes in the field and brought them to his mother Leah. Then Rachel said to Leah, "Please give me some of your son's mandrakes." 15 But she said to her, "Is it a small matter that you have taken away my husband? Would you take away my son's mandrakes also?" Rachel said, "Then he may lie with you tonight in exchange for your son's mandrakes." 16 When Jacob came from the field in the evening, Leah went out to meet him and said, "You must come in to me, for I have hired you with my son's mandrakes." So he lay with her that night. 17 And God listened to Leah, and she

LESSON 3:
JACOB'S BATTLE OF THE FLESH, EXPERIENCE OF VICTORY OVER THE FLESH, GOD'S FAITHFULNESS DESPITE THE FLESH

> conceived and bore Jacob a fifth son. [18] Leah said, "God has given me my wages because I gave my servant to my husband." So she called his name Issachar.[l]
>
> [19] And Leah conceived again, and she bore Jacob a sixth son. [20] Then Leah said, "God has endowed me with a good endowment; now my husband will honor me, because I have borne him six sons." So she called his name Zebulun.[m] [21] Afterward she bore a daughter and called her name Dinah.
>
> [22] Then God remembered Rachel, and God listened to her and opened her womb. [23] She conceived and bore a son and said, "God has taken away my reproach." [24] And she called his name Joseph,[n] saying, "May the Lord add to me another son!"

_____
_____
_____
_____
_____

Read through these verses and write out the reasons Laban wanted Jacob to stay with him. What did Laban try to do to keep Jacob and/or not have Jacob be blessed? What did God do in this situation? Why? And why is this so significant to us?

> **Read Genesis 30:25–31:13:**
>
> Jacob's Prosperity
>
> [25] As soon as Rachel had borne Joseph, Jacob said to Laban, "Send me away, that I may go to my own home and country. [26] Give me my wives and my children for whom I have served you, that I may go, for you know the service that I have given you." [27] But Laban said to him, "If I have found favor in your sight, I have learned by divination that[a] the Lord has blessed me because of you. [28] Name your wages, and I will give it." [29] Jacob said to him, "You yourself know how I have served you, and how your livestock has fared with me. [30] For you had little before I came, and it has increased abundantly, and the Lord has blessed you wherever I turned. But now when shall I provide for my own household also?" [31] He said, "What shall I give you?" Jacob said, "You shall not give me anything. If you will do this for me, I will again pasture your

LESSON 3:
JACOB'S BATTLE OF THE FLESH, EXPERIENCE OF VICTORY OVER THE FLESH, GOD'S FAITHFULNESS DESPITE THE FLESH

flock and keep it: 32 let me pass through all your flock today, removing from it every speckled and spotted sheep and every black lamb, and the spotted and speckled among the goats, and they shall be my wages. 33 So my honesty will answer for me later, when you come to look into my wages with you. Every one that is not speckled and spotted among the goats and black among the lambs, if found with me, shall be counted stolen." 34 Laban said, "Good! Let it be as you have said." 35 But that day Laban removed the male goats that were striped and spotted, and all the female goats that were speckled and spotted, every one that had white on it, and every lamb that was black, and put them in the charge of his sons. 36 And he set a distance of three days' journey between himself and Jacob, and Jacob pastured the rest of Laban's flock.

37 Then Jacob took fresh sticks of poplar and almond and plane trees, and peeled white streaks in them, exposing the white of the sticks. 38 He set the sticks that he had peeled in front of the flocks in the troughs, that is, the watering places, where the flocks came to drink. And since they bred when they came to drink, 39 the flocks bred in front of the sticks and so the flocks brought forth striped, speckled, and spotted. 40 And Jacob separated the lambs and set the faces of the flocks toward the striped and all the black in the flock of Laban. He put his own droves apart and did not put them with Laban's flock. 41 Whenever the stronger of the flock were breeding, Jacob would lay the sticks in the troughs before the eyes of the flock, that they might breed among the sticks, 42 but for the feebler of the flock he would not lay them there. So the feebler would be Laban's, and the stronger Jacob's. 43 Thus the man increased greatly and had large flocks, female servants and male servants, and camels and donkeys.

Jacob Flees from Laban

31 Now Jacob heard that the sons of Laban were saying, "Jacob has taken all that was our father's, and from what was our father's he has gained all this wealth." 2 And Jacob saw that Laban did not regard him with favor as before. 3 Then the Lord said to Jacob, "Return to the land of your fathers and to your kindred, and I will be with you."

4 So Jacob sent and called Rachel and Leah into the field where his flock was 5 and said to them, "I see that your father does not regard me with favor as he did before. But the God of my father has been with me. 6 You know that I have served your father with all my strength, 7 yet your father has cheated me

LESSON 3:
JACOB'S BATTLE OF THE FLESH, EXPERIENCE OF VICTORY OVER THE FLESH, GOD'S FAITHFULNESS DESPITE THE FLESH

> and changed my wages ten times. But God did not permit him to harm me. [8] If he said, 'The spotted shall be your wages,' then all the flock bore spotted; and if he said, 'The striped shall be your wages,' then all the flock bore striped. [9] Thus God has taken away the livestock of your father and given them to me. [10] In the breeding season of the flock I lifted up my eyes and saw in a dream that the goats that mated with the flock were striped, spotted, and mottled. [11] Then the angel of God said to me in the dream, 'Jacob,' and I said, 'Here I am!' [12] And he said, 'Lift up your eyes and see, all the goats that mate with the flock are striped, spotted, and mottled, for I have seen all that Laban is doing to you. [13] I am the God of Bethel, where you anointed a pillar and made a vow to me. Now arise, go out from this land and return to the land of your kindred.'"

_____
_____
_____
_____
_____

Read through these verses and write down what Jacob did by leaving Laban. What caused him to operate this way, and how did God intervene to fulfill His purposes? Why is this so significant to us?

> **Read Genesis 31:14–55:**
>
> [14] Then Rachel and Leah answered and said to him, "Is there any portion or inheritance left to us in our father's house? [15] Are we not regarded by him as foreigners? For he has sold us, and he has indeed devoured our money. [16] All the wealth that God has taken away from our father belongs to us and to our children. Now then, whatever God has said to you, do."
>
> [17] So Jacob arose and set his sons and his wives on camels. [18] He drove away all his livestock, all his property that he had gained, the livestock in his possession that he had acquired in Paddan-aram, to go to the land of Canaan to his father Isaac. [19] Laban had gone to shear his sheep, and Rachel stole her father's household gods. [20] And Jacob tricked[a] Laban the Aramean, by not

LESSON 3:
JACOB'S BATTLE OF THE FLESH, EXPERIENCE OF VICTORY OVER THE FLESH, GOD'S FAITHFULNESS DESPITE THE FLESH

telling him that he intended to flee. ²¹ He fled with all that he had and arose and crossed the Euphrates,[b] and set his face toward the hill country of Gilead.

²² When it was told Laban on the third day that Jacob had fled, ²³ he took his kinsmen with him and pursued him for seven days and followed close after him into the hill country of Gilead. ²⁴ But God came to Laban the Aramean in a dream by night and said to him, "Be careful not to say anything to Jacob, either good or bad."

²⁵ And Laban overtook Jacob. Now Jacob had pitched his tent in the hill country, and Laban with his kinsmen pitched tents in the hill country of Gilead. ²⁶ And Laban said to Jacob, "What have you done, that you have tricked me and driven away my daughters like captives of the sword? ²⁷ Why did you flee secretly and trick me, and did not tell me, so that I might have sent you away with mirth and songs, with tambourine and lyre? ²⁸ And why did you not permit me to kiss my sons and my daughters farewell? Now you have done foolishly. ²⁹ It is in my power to do you harm. But the God of your[c] father spoke to me last night, saying, 'Be careful not to say anything to Jacob, either good or bad.' ³⁰ And now you have gone away because you longed greatly for your father's house, but why did you steal my gods?" ³¹ Jacob answered and said to Laban, "Because I was afraid, for I thought that you would take your daughters from me by force. ³² Anyone with whom you find your gods shall not live. In the presence of our kinsmen point out what I have that is yours, and take it." Now Jacob did not know that Rachel had stolen them.

³³ So Laban went into Jacob's tent and into Leah's tent and into the tent of the two female servants, but he did not find them. And he went out of Leah's tent and entered Rachel's. ³⁴ Now Rachel had taken the household gods and put them in the camel's saddle and sat on them. Laban felt all about the tent, but did not find them. ³⁵ And she said to her father, "Let not my lord be angry that I cannot rise before you, for the way of women is upon me." So he searched but did not find the household gods.

³⁶ Then Jacob became angry and berated Laban. Jacob said to Laban, "What is my offense? What is my sin, that you have hotly pursued me? ³⁷ For you have felt through all my goods; what have you found of all your household goods? Set it here before my kinsmen and your kinsmen, that they may decide between us two. ³⁸ These twenty years I have been with you. Your ewes and your female goats have not miscarried, and I have not eaten the rams of your flocks. ³⁹ What was torn by wild beasts I did not bring to you. I bore the loss of it myself. From my hand you required it, whether stolen by day or stolen by night. ⁴⁰ There I was:

LESSON 3:
JACOB'S BATTLE OF THE FLESH, EXPERIENCE OF VICTORY OVER THE FLESH, GOD'S FAITHFULNESS DESPITE THE FLESH

by day the heat consumed me, and the cold by night, and my sleep fled from my eyes. ⁴¹ These twenty years I have been in your house. I served you fourteen years for your two daughters, and six years for your flock, and you have changed my wages ten times. ⁴² If the God of my father, the God of Abraham and the Fear of Isaac, had not been on my side, surely now you would have sent me away empty-handed. God saw my affliction and the labor of my hands and rebuked you last night."

⁴³ Then Laban answered and said to Jacob, "The daughters are my daughters, the children are my children, the flocks are my flocks, and all that you see is mine. But what can I do this day for these my daughters or for their children whom they have borne? ⁴⁴ Come now, let us make a covenant, you and I. And let it be a witness between you and me." ⁴⁵ So Jacob took a stone and set it up as a pillar. ⁴⁶ And Jacob said to his kinsmen, "Gather stones." And they took stones and made a heap, and they ate there by the heap. ⁴⁷ Laban called it Jegar-sahadutha,[d] but Jacob called it Galeed.[e] ⁴⁸ Laban said, "This heap is a witness between you and me today." Therefore he named it Galeed, ⁴⁹ and Mizpah,[f] for he said, "The Lord watch between you and me, when we are out of one another's sight. ⁵⁰ If you oppress my daughters, or if you take wives besides my daughters, although no one is with us, see, God is witness between you and me."

⁵¹ Then Laban said to Jacob, "See this heap and the pillar, which I have set between you and me. ⁵² This heap is a witness, and the pillar is a witness, that I will not pass over this heap to you, and you will not pass over this heap and this pillar to me, to do harm. ⁵³ The God of Abraham and the God of Nahor, the God of their father, judge between us." So Jacob swore by the Fear of his father Isaac, ⁵⁴ and Jacob offered a sacrifice in the hill country and called his kinsmen to eat bread. They ate bread and spent the night in the hill country.

⁵⁵ [g] Early in the morning Laban arose and kissed his grandchildren and his daughters and blessed them. Then Laban departed and returned home.

_____
_____
_____
_____
_____

LESSON 4: JACOB'S WRESTLING WITH GOD AS HE UNDERSTANDS SURRENDER; ISRAEL'S CONTINUED BATTLE WITH THE FLESH/ THE ENEMY (ESAU'S DESCENDANTS)

Read through these verses and write out how Jacob approached meeting Esau. Why did he operate this way? What actually happened in Jacob's encounter with God? What did this show Jacob and thus, what is the importance to how we live?

> **Read Genesis 32:1–33:19:**
>
> Jacob Fears Esau
>
> **32** Jacob went on his way, and the angels of God met him. ² And when Jacob saw them he said, "This is God's camp!" So he called the name of that place Mahanaim.[a]
>
> ³ And Jacob sent[b] messengers before him to Esau his brother in the land of Seir, the country of Edom, ⁴ instructing them, "Thus you shall say to my lord Esau: Thus says your servant Jacob, 'I have sojourned with Laban and stayed until now. ⁵ I have oxen, donkeys, flocks, male servants, and female servants. I have sent to tell my lord, in order that I may find favor in your sight.'"
>
> ⁶ And the messengers returned to Jacob, saying, "We came to your brother Esau, and he is coming to meet you, and there are four hundred men with him." ⁷ Then Jacob was greatly afraid and distressed. He divided the people who were with him, and the flocks and herds and camels, into two camps, ⁸ thinking, "If Esau comes to the one camp and attacks it, then the camp that is left will escape."
>
> ⁹ And Jacob said, "O God of my father Abraham and God of my father Isaac, O Lord who said to me, 'Return to your country and to your kindred, that I may do you good,' ¹⁰ I am not worthy of the least of all the deeds of steadfast love and all the faithfulness that you have shown to your servant, for with only my staff I crossed this Jordan, and now I have become two camps. ¹¹ Please deliver me from the hand of my brother, from the hand of Esau, for I fear him, that he may come and attack me, the mothers with the children. ¹² But you said, 'I will surely do you good, and make your offspring as the sand of the sea, which cannot be numbered for multitude.'"

> "Because of the default position of our nature, we go to self. And no matter what we try to do, even good things, we can't fulfill it on our own."

LESSON 4: JACOB'S WRESTLING WITH GOD AS HE UNDERSTANDS SURRENDER; ISRAEL'S CONTINUED BATTLE WITH THE FLESH/ THE ENEMY (ESAU'S DESCENDANTS)

13 So he stayed there that night, and from what he had with him he took a present for his brother Esau, 14 two hundred female goats and twenty male goats, two hundred ewes and twenty rams, 15 thirty milking camels and their calves, forty cows and ten bulls, twenty female donkeys and ten male donkeys. 16 These he handed over to his servants, every drove by itself, and said to his servants, "Pass on ahead of me and put a space between drove and drove." 17 He instructed the first, "When Esau my brother meets you and asks you, 'To whom do you belong? Where are you going? And whose are these ahead of you?' 18 then you shall say, 'They belong to your servant Jacob. They are a present sent to my lord Esau. And moreover, he is behind us.'" 19 He likewise instructed the second and the third and all who followed the droves, "You shall say the same thing to Esau when you find him, 20 and you shall say, 'Moreover, your servant Jacob is behind us.'" For he thought, "I may appease him[c] with the present that goes ahead of me, and afterward I shall see his face. Perhaps he will accept me."[d] 21 So the present passed on ahead of him, and he himself stayed that night in the camp.

Jacob Wrestles with God

22 The same night he arose and took his two wives, his two female servants, and his eleven children,[e] and crossed the ford of the Jabbok. 23 He took them and sent them across the stream, and everything else that he had. 24 And Jacob was left alone. And a man wrestled with him until the breaking of the day. 25 When the man saw that he did not prevail against Jacob, he touched his hip socket, and Jacob's hip was put out of joint as he wrestled with him. 26 Then he said, "Let me go, for the day has broken." But Jacob said, "I will not let you go unless you bless me." 27 And he said to him, "What is your name?" And he said, "Jacob." 28 Then he said, "Your name shall no longer be called Jacob, but Israel,[f] for you have striven with God and with men, and have prevailed." 29 Then Jacob asked him, "Please tell me your name." But he said, "Why is it that you ask my name?" And there he blessed him. 30 So Jacob called the name of the place Peniel,[g] saying, "For I have seen God face to face, and yet my life has been delivered." 31 The sun rose upon him as he passed Penuel, limping because of his hip. 32 Therefore to this day the people of Israel do not eat the sinew of the thigh that is on the hip socket, because he touched the socket of Jacob's hip on the sinew of the thigh.

LESSON 4: JACOB'S WRESTLING WITH GOD AS HE UNDERSTANDS SURRENDER; ISRAEL'S CONTINUED BATTLE WITH THE FLESH/ THE ENEMY (ESAU'S DESCENDANTS)

Jacob Meets Esau

33 And Jacob lifted up his eyes and looked, and behold, Esau was coming, and four hundred men with him. So he divided the children among Leah and Rachel and the two female servants. ² And he put the servants with their children in front, then Leah with her children, and Rachel and Joseph last of all. ³ He himself went on before them, bowing himself to the ground seven times, until he came near to his brother.

⁴ But Esau ran to meet him and embraced him and fell on his neck and kissed him, and they wept. ⁵ And when Esau lifted up his eyes and saw the women and children, he said, "Who are these with you?" Jacob said, "The children whom God has graciously given your servant." ⁶ Then the servants drew near, they and their children, and bowed down. ⁷ Leah likewise and her children drew near and bowed down. And last Joseph and Rachel drew near, and they bowed down. ⁸ Esau said, "What do you mean by all this company[h] that I met?" Jacob answered, "To find favor in the sight of my lord." ⁹ But Esau said, "I have enough, my brother; keep what you have for yourself." ¹⁰ Jacob said, "No, please, if I have found favor in your sight, then accept my present from my hand. For I have seen your face, which is like seeing the face of God, and you have accepted me. ¹¹ Please accept my blessing that is brought to you, because God has dealt graciously with me, and because I have enough." Thus he urged him, and he took it.

¹² Then Esau said, "Let us journey on our way, and I will go ahead of[i] you." ¹³ But Jacob said to him, "My lord knows that the children are frail, and that the nursing flocks and herds are a care to me. If they are driven hard for one day, all the flocks will die. ¹⁴ Let my lord pass on ahead of his servant, and I will lead on slowly, at the pace of the livestock that are ahead of me and at the pace of the children, until I come to my lord in Seir."

¹⁵ So Esau said, "Let me leave with you some of the people who are with me." But he said, "What need is there? Let me find favor in the sight of my lord." ¹⁶ So Esau returned that day on his way to Seir. ¹⁷ But Jacob journeyed to Succoth, and built himself a house and made booths for his livestock. Therefore the name of the place is called Succoth.[j]

¹⁸ And Jacob came safely[k] to the city of Shechem, which is in the land of Canaan, on his way from Paddan-aram, and he camped before the city. ¹⁹ And from the sons of Hamor, Shechem's father, he bought for a hundred pieces of money[l] the piece of land on which he had pitched his tent.

LESSON 4: JACOB'S WRESTLING WITH GOD AS HE UNDERSTANDS SURRENDER; ISRAEL'S CONTINUED BATTLE WITH THE FLESH/ THE ENEMY (ESAU'S DESCENDANTS)

_____
_____
_____
_____
_____

Read through these sets of verses and write out how and why we are to "wrestle things out with God." Why is this so important and a requirement for living in the Spirit versus the flesh?

> **Read John 4:34:**
>
> ³⁴ Jesus said to them, "My food is to do the will of him who sent me and to accomplish his work.

_____
_____
_____
_____
_____

> **Read John 6:38:**
>
> ³⁸ For I have come down from heaven, not to do my own will but the will of him who sent me.

_____
_____
_____
_____
_____

LESSON 4: JACOB'S WRESTLING WITH GOD AS HE UNDERSTANDS SURRENDER; ISRAEL'S CONTINUED BATTLE WITH THE FLESH/ THE ENEMY (ESAU'S DESCENDANTS)

Read John 10:17–18:

17 For this reason the Father loves me, because I lay down my life that I may take it up again. 18 No one takes it from me, but I lay it down of my own accord. I have authority to lay it down, and I have authority to take it up again. This charge I have received from my Father."

_____
_____
_____
_____

Read John 15:1–8:

I Am the True Vine

15 "I am the true vine, and my Father is the vinedresser. 2 Every branch in me that does not bear fruit he takes away, and every branch that does bear fruit he prunes, that it may bear more fruit. 3 Already you are clean because of the word that I have spoken to you. 4 Abide in me, and I in you. As the branch cannot bear fruit by itself, unless it abides in the vine, neither can you, unless you abide in me. 5 I am the vine; you are the branches. Whoever abides in me and I in him, he it is that bears much fruit, for apart from me you can do nothing. 6 If anyone does not abide in me he is thrown away like a branch and withers; and the branches are gathered, thrown into the fire, and burned. 7 If you abide in me, and my words abide in you, ask whatever you wish, and it will be done for you. 8 By this my Father is glorified, that you bear much fruit and so prove to be my disciples.

_____
_____
_____
_____

LESSON 4: JACOB'S WRESTLING WITH GOD AS HE UNDERSTANDS SURRENDER; ISRAEL'S CONTINUED BATTLE WITH THE FLESH/ THE ENEMY (ESAU'S DESCENDANTS)

Read through these verses and write out the promise given to Jacob and the significance to us as believers. What is God's story that is being revealed, and why is it so significant to us?

> **Read Genesis 35:1–36:13:**
>
> God Blesses and Renames Jacob
> **35** God said to Jacob, "Arise, go up to Bethel and dwell there. Make an altar there to the God who appeared to you when you fled from your brother Esau." 2 So Jacob said to his household and to all who were with him, "Put away the foreign gods that are among you and purify yourselves and change your garments. 3 Then let us arise and go up to Bethel, so that I may make there an altar to the God who answers me in the day of my distress and has been with me wherever I have gone." 4 So they gave to Jacob all the foreign gods that they had, and the rings that were in their ears. Jacob hid them under the terebinth tree that was near Shechem.
>
> 5 And as they journeyed, a terror from God fell upon the cities that were around them, so that they did not pursue the sons of Jacob. 6 And Jacob came to Luz (that is, Bethel), which is in the land of Canaan, he and all the people who were with him, 7 and there he built an altar and called the place El-bethel,[a] because there God had revealed himself to him when he fled from his brother. 8 And Deborah, Rebekah's nurse, died, and she was buried under an oak below Bethel. So he called its name Allon-bacuth.[b]
>
> 9 God appeared[c] to Jacob again, when he came from Paddan-aram, and blessed him. 10 And God said to him, "Your name is Jacob; no longer shall your name be called Jacob, but Israel shall be your name." So he called his name Israel. 11 And God said to him, "I am God Almighty:[d] be fruitful and multiply. A nation and a company of nations shall come from you, and kings shall come from your own body.[e] 12 The land that I gave to Abraham and Isaac I will give to you, and I will give the land to your offspring after you." 13 Then God went up from him in the place where he had spoken with him. 14 And Jacob set up a pillar in the place where he had spoken with him, a pillar of stone. He poured out a drink offering on it and poured oil on it. 15 So Jacob called the name of the place where God had spoken with him Bethel.
>
> The Deaths of Rachel and Isaac
> 16 Then they journeyed from Bethel. When they were still some distance[f] from Ephrath, Rachel went into labor, and she had hard labor. 17 And when her labor

LESSON 4: JACOB'S WRESTLING WITH GOD AS HE UNDERSTANDS SURRENDER; ISRAEL'S CONTINUED BATTLE WITH THE FLESH/ THE ENEMY (ESAU'S DESCENDANTS)

was at its hardest, the midwife said to her, "Do not fear, for you have another son." [18] And as her soul was departing (for she was dying), she called his name Ben-oni;[g] but his father called him Benjamin.[h] [19] So Rachel died, and she was buried on the way to Ephrath (that is, Bethlehem), [20] and Jacob set up a pillar over her tomb. It is the pillar of Rachel's tomb, which is there to this day. [21] Israel journeyed on and pitched his tent beyond the tower of Eder.

[22] While Israel lived in that land, Reuben went and lay with Bilhah his father's concubine. And Israel heard of it.

Now the sons of Jacob were twelve. [23] The sons of Leah: Reuben (Jacob's firstborn), Simeon, Levi, Judah, Issachar, and Zebulun. [24] The sons of Rachel: Joseph and Benjamin. [25] The sons of Bilhah, Rachel's servant: Dan and Naphtali. [26] The sons of Zilpah, Leah's servant: Gad and Asher. These were the sons of Jacob who were born to him in Paddan-aram.

[27] And Jacob came to his father Isaac at Mamre, or Kiriath-arba (that is, Hebron), where Abraham and Isaac had sojourned. [28] Now the days of Isaac were 180 years. [29] And Isaac breathed his last, and he died and was gathered to his people, old and full of days. And his sons Esau and Jacob buried him.

Esau's Descendants
36 These are the generations of Esau (that is, Edom). [2] Esau took his wives from the Canaanites: Adah the daughter of Elon the Hittite, Oholibamah the daughter of Anah the daughter[i] of Zibeon the Hivite, [3] and Basemath, Ishmael's daughter, the sister of Nebaioth. [4] And Adah bore to Esau, Eliphaz; Basemath bore Reuel; [5] and Oholibamah bore Jeush, Jalam, and Korah. These are the sons of Esau who were born to him in the land of Canaan.

[6] Then Esau took his wives, his sons, his daughters, and all the members of his household, his livestock, all his beasts, and all his property that he had acquired in the land of Canaan. He went into a land away from his brother Jacob. [7] For their possessions were too great for them to dwell together. The land of their sojournings could not support them because of their livestock. [8] So Esau settled in the hill country of Seir. (Esau is Edom.)

[9] These are the generations of Esau the father of the Edomites in the hill country of Seir. [10] These are the names of Esau's sons: Eliphaz the son of Adah the wife of Esau, Reuel the son of Basemath the wife of Esau. [11] The sons of Eliphaz were Teman, Omar, Zepho, Gatam, and Kenaz. [12] (Timna was a concubine of Eliphaz, Esau's son; she bore Amalek to Eliphaz.) These are the sons of Adah, Esau's wife. [13] These are the sons of Reuel: Nahath, Zerah, Shammah, and Mizzah. These are the sons of Basemath, Esau's wife.

LESSON 4: JACOB'S WRESTLING WITH GOD AS HE UNDERSTANDS SURRENDER; ISRAEL'S CONTINUED BATTLE WITH THE FLESH/ THE ENEMY (ESAU'S DESCENDANTS)

_____
_____
_____
_____
_____

Read through these verses and write out the significance of the Amalekites and how they still impact our lives today. How are we to respond to the enemy? What does this provide for us? Why is this so significant for us?

> **Read Exodus 17:8–16:**
>
> Israel Defeats Amalek
> [8] Then Amalek came and fought with Israel at Rephidim. [9] So Moses said to Joshua, "Choose for us men, and go out and fight with Amalek. Tomorrow I will stand on the top of the hill with the staff of God in my hand." [10] So Joshua did as Moses told him, and fought with Amalek, while Moses, Aaron, and Hur went up to the top of the hill. [11] Whenever Moses held up his hand, Israel prevailed, and whenever he lowered his hand, Amalek prevailed. [12] But Moses' hands grew weary, so they took a stone and put it under him, and he sat on it, while Aaron and Hur held up his hands, one on one side, and the other on the other side. So his hands were steady until the going down of the sun. [13] And Joshua overwhelmed Amalek and his people with the sword.
> [14] Then the Lord said to Moses, "Write this as a memorial in a book and recite it in the ears of Joshua, that I will utterly blot out the memory of Amalek from under heaven." [15] And Moses built an altar and called the name of it, The Lord Is My Banner, [16] saying, "A hand upon the throne[a] of the Lord! The Lord will have war with Amalek from generation to generation."

_____
_____
_____
_____
_____

LESSON 4: JACOB'S WRESTLING WITH GOD AS HE UNDERSTANDS SURRENDER; ISRAEL'S CONTINUED BATTLE WITH THE FLESH/ THE ENEMY (ESAU'S DESCENDANTS)

Read through these sets of verses and write out what happened with Balaam. What does this mean for us today?

Read Numbers 22:1–41:

Balak Summons Balaam

22 Then the people of Israel set out and camped in the plains of Moab beyond the Jordan at Jericho. ² And Balak the son of Zippor saw all that Israel had done to the Amorites. ³ And Moab was in great dread of the people, because they were many. Moab was overcome with fear of the people of Israel. ⁴ And Moab said to the elders of Midian, "This horde will now lick up all that is around us, as the ox licks up the grass of the field." So Balak the son of Zippor, who was king of Moab at that time, ⁵ sent messengers to Balaam the son of Beor at Pethor, which is near the River[a] in the land of the people of Amaw,[b] to call him, saying, "Behold, a people has come out of Egypt. They cover the face of the earth, and they are dwelling opposite me. ⁶ Come now, curse this people for me, since they are too mighty for me. Perhaps I shall be able to defeat them and drive them from the land, for I know that he whom you bless is blessed, and he whom you curse is cursed."

⁷ So the elders of Moab and the elders of Midian departed with the fees for divination in their hand. And they came to Balaam and gave him Balak's message. ⁸ And he said to them, "Lodge here tonight, and I will bring back word to you, as the Lord speaks to me." So the princes of Moab stayed with Balaam. ⁹ And God came to Balaam and said, "Who are these men with you?" ¹⁰ And Balaam said to God, "Balak the son of Zippor, king of Moab, has sent to me, saying, ¹¹ 'Behold, a people has come out of Egypt, and it covers the face of the earth. Now come, curse them for me. Perhaps I shall be able to fight against them and drive them out.'" ¹² God said to Balaam, "You shall not go with them. You shall not curse the people, for they are blessed." ¹³ So Balaam rose in the morning and said to the princes of Balak, "Go to your own land, for the Lord has refused to let me go with you." ¹⁴ So the princes of Moab rose and went to Balak and said, "Balaam refuses to come with us."

¹⁵ Once again Balak sent princes, more in number and more honorable than these. ¹⁶ And they came to Balaam and said to him, "Thus says Balak the son of Zippor: 'Let nothing hinder you from coming to me, ¹⁷ for I will surely do you great honor, and whatever you say to me I will do. Come, curse this people for me.'" ¹⁸ But Balaam answered and said to the servants of Balak, "Though Balak were to give me his house full of silver and gold, I could not go beyond the

LESSON 4: JACOB'S WRESTLING WITH GOD AS HE UNDERSTANDS SURRENDER; ISRAEL'S CONTINUED BATTLE WITH THE FLESH/ THE ENEMY (ESAU'S DESCENDANTS)

command of the Lord my God to do less or more. [19] So you, too, please stay here tonight, that I may know what more the Lord will say to me." [20] And God came to Balaam at night and said to him, "If the men have come to call you, rise, go with them; but only do what I tell you." [21] So Balaam rose in the morning and saddled his donkey and went with the princes of Moab.

Balaam's Donkey and the Angel
[22] But God's anger was kindled because he went, and the angel of the Lord took his stand in the way as his adversary. Now he was riding on the donkey, and his two servants were with him. [23] And the donkey saw the angel of the Lord standing in the road, with a drawn sword in his hand. And the donkey turned aside out of the road and went into the field. And Balaam struck the donkey, to turn her into the road. [24] Then the angel of the Lord stood in a narrow path between the vineyards, with a wall on either side. [25] And when the donkey saw the angel of the Lord, she pushed against the wall and pressed Balaam's foot against the wall. So he struck her again. [26] Then the angel of the Lord went ahead and stood in a narrow place, where there was no way to turn either to the right or to the left. [27] When the donkey saw the angel of the Lord, she lay down under Balaam. And Balaam's anger was kindled, and he struck the donkey with his staff. [28] Then the Lord opened the mouth of the donkey, and she said to Balaam, "What have I done to you, that you have struck me these three times?" [29] And Balaam said to the donkey, "Because you have made a fool of me. I wish I had a sword in my hand, for then I would kill you." [30] And the donkey said to Balaam, "Am I not your donkey, on which you have ridden all your life long to this day? Is it my habit to treat you this way?" And he said, "No."

[31] Then the Lord opened the eyes of Balaam, and he saw the angel of the Lord standing in the way, with his drawn sword in his hand. And he bowed down and fell on his face. [32] And the angel of the Lord said to him, "Why have you struck your donkey these three times? Behold, I have come out to oppose you because your way is perverse[c] before me. [33] The donkey saw me and turned aside before me these three times. If she had not turned aside from me, surely just now I would have killed you and let her live." [34] Then Balaam said to the angel of the Lord, "I have sinned, for I did not know that you stood in the road against me. Now therefore, if it is evil in your sight, I will turn back." [35] And the angel of the Lord said to Balaam, "Go with the men, but speak only the word that I tell you." So Balaam went on with the princes of Balak.

LESSON 4: JACOB'S WRESTLING WITH GOD AS HE UNDERSTANDS SURRENDER; ISRAEL'S CONTINUED BATTLE WITH THE FLESH/ THE ENEMY (ESAU'S DESCENDANTS)

> 36 When Balak heard that Balaam had come, he went out to meet him at the city of Moab, on the border formed by the Arnon, at the extremity of the border. 37 And Balak said to Balaam, "Did I not send to you to call you? Why did you not come to me? Am I not able to honor you?" 38 Balaam said to Balak, "Behold, I have come to you! Have I now any power of my own to speak anything? The word that God puts in my mouth, that must I speak." 39 Then Balaam went with Balak, and they came to Kiriath-huzoth. 40 And Balak sacrificed oxen and sheep, and sent for Balaam and for the princes who were with him.
>
> 41 And in the morning Balak took Balaam and brought him up to Bamoth-baal, and from there he saw a fraction of the people.

_____

Read Numbers 23:11–12:

> 11 And Balak said to Balaam, "What have you done to me? I took you to curse my enemies, and behold, you have done nothing but bless them." 12 And he answered and said, "Must I not take care to speak what the Lord puts in my mouth?"

_____

LESSON 4: JACOB'S WRESTLING WITH GOD AS HE UNDERSTANDS SURRENDER; ISRAEL'S CONTINUED BATTLE WITH THE FLESH/ THE ENEMY (ESAU'S DESCENDANTS)

> **Read Numbers 23:25–26:**
>
> ²⁵ And Balak said to Balaam, "Do not curse them at all, and do not bless them at all." ²⁶ But Balaam answered Balak, "Did I not tell you, 'All that the Lord says, that I must do'?"

_____

_____

_____

_____

_____

> **Read Numbers 24:10–14:**
>
> ¹⁰ And Balak's anger was kindled against Balaam, and he struck his hands together. And Balak said to Balaam, "I called you to curse my enemies, and behold, you have blessed them these three times. ¹¹ Therefore now flee to your own place. I said, 'I will certainly honor you,' but the Lord has held you back from honor." ¹² And Balaam said to Balak, "Did I not tell your messengers whom you sent to me, ¹³ 'If Balak should give me his house full of silver and gold, I would not be able to go beyond the word of the Lord, to do either good or bad of my own will. What the Lord speaks, that will I speak'? ¹⁴ And now, behold, I am going to my people. Come, I will let you know what this people will do to your people in the latter days."

_____

_____

_____

_____

_____

LESSON 5:
HOW WE LIFE IN THE SPIRIT AND EXPERIENCE GOD'S POWER OVER THE FLESH AND THE ENEMY

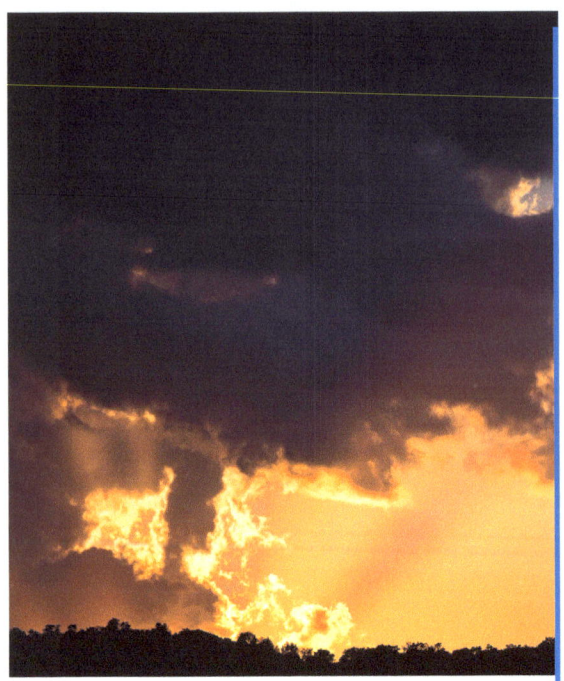

Read through these verses and write out the principles that we are to receive regarding what was revealed to Balaam and the significance it has to us today.

> **Read Numbers 24:15–25:**
>
> Balaam's Final Oracle
> [15] And he took up his discourse and said,
>
> "The oracle of Balaam the son of Beor,
>   the oracle of the man whose eye is opened,
> [16] the oracle of him who hears the words of God,
>   and knows the knowledge of the Most High,
> who sees the vision of the Almighty,
>   falling down with his eyes uncovered:
> [17] I see him, but not now;
>   I behold him, but not near:
> a star shall come out of Jacob,
>   and a scepter shall rise out of Israel;
> it shall crush the forehead[a] of Moab
>   and break down all the sons of Sheth.
> [18] Edom shall be dispossessed;
>   Seir also, his enemies, shall be dispossessed.
>   Israel is doing valiantly.
> [19] And one from Jacob shall exercise dominion
>   and destroy the survivors of cities!"
>
> [20] Then he looked on Amalek and took up his discourse and said,
> "Amalek was the first among the nations,
>   but its end is utter destruction."
>
> [21] And he looked on the Kenite, and took up his discourse and said,
> "Enduring is your dwelling place,
>   and your nest is set in the rock.
> [22] Nevertheless, Kain shall be burned
>   when Asshur takes you away captive."
>
> [23] And he took up his discourse and said,
> "Alas, who shall live when God does this?
> [24] But ships shall come from Kittim

> "Remember, the sin isn't the act in which you are engaged. It's walking in the flesh. It may translate into addiction, fear, anxiety, worry, anger."

LESSON 5:
HOW WE LIFE IN THE SPIRIT AND EXPERIENCE GOD'S POWER OVER THE FLESH AND THE ENEMY

> and shall afflict Asshur and Eber;
> and he too shall come to utter destruction."
>
> 25 Then Balaam rose and went back to his place. And Balak also went his way.

_____
_____
_____
_____
_____

Read through these sets of verses and write out the basis by which we are protected. How then should we proceed when attacked by the enemy? Why is this so important to us in our everyday lives?

> **Read Colossians 2:11–15:**
>
> 11 In him also you were circumcised with a circumcision made without hands, by putting off the body of the flesh, by the circumcision of Christ, 12 having been buried with him in baptism, in which you were also raised with him through faith in the powerful working of God, who raised him from the dead. 13 And you, who were dead in your trespasses and the uncircumcision of your flesh, God made alive together with him, having forgiven us all our trespasses, 14 by canceling the record of debt that stood against us with its legal demands. This he set aside, nailing it to the cross. 15 He disarmed the rulers and authorities[a] and put them to open shame, by triumphing over them in him.[b]

_____
_____
_____
_____
_____

LESSON 5:
HOW WE LIFE IN THE SPIRIT AND EXPERIENCE GOD'S POWER OVER THE FLESH AND THE ENEMY

> **Read Deuteronomy 25:17–19:**
>
> [17] "Remember what Amalek did to you on the way as you came out of Egypt, [18] how he attacked you on the way when you were faint and weary, and cut off your tail, those who were lagging behind you, and he did not fear God. [19] Therefore when the Lord your God has given you rest from all your enemies around you, in the land that the Lord your God is giving you for an inheritance to possess, you shall blot out the memory of Amalek from under heaven; you shall not forget.

_____
_____
_____
_____

> **Read Judges 6:1–6:**
>
> Midian Oppresses Israel
> **6** The people of Israel did what was evil in the sight of the Lord, and the Lord gave them into the hand of Midian seven years. [2] And the hand of Midian overpowered Israel, and because of Midian the people of Israel made for themselves the dens that are in the mountains and the caves and the strongholds. [3] For whenever the Israelites planted crops, the Midianites and the Amalekites and the people of the East would come up against them. [4] They would encamp against them and devour the produce of the land, as far as Gaza, and leave no sustenance in Israel and no sheep or ox or donkey. [5] For they would come up with their livestock and their tents; they would come like locusts in number—both they and their camels could not be counted—so that they laid waste the land as they came in. [6] And Israel was brought very low because of Midian. And the people of Israel cried out for help to the Lord.

LESSON 5:
HOW WE LIFE IN THE SPIRIT AND EXPERIENCE GOD'S POWER OVER THE FLESH AND THE ENEMY

> **Read Ephesians 6:10–13:**
>
> The Whole Armor of God
> [10] Finally, be strong in the Lord and in the strength of his might. [11] Put on the whole armor of God, that you may be able to stand against the schemes of the devil. [12] For we do not wrestle against flesh and blood, but against the rulers, against the authorities, against the cosmic powers over this present darkness, against the spiritual forces of evil in the heavenly places. [13] Therefore take up the whole armor of God, that you may be able to withstand in the evil day, and having done all, to stand firm.

_____
_____
_____
_____
_____

> **Read 1 Peter 5:8:**
>
> [8] Be sober-minded; be watchful. Your adversary the devil prowls around like a roaring lion, seeking someone to devour.

_____
_____
_____
_____
_____

LESSON 5:
HOW WE LIFE IN THE SPIRIT AND EXPERIENCE GOD'S POWER OVER THE FLESH AND THE ENEMY

Read James 1:12–18:

12 Blessed is the man who remains steadfast under trial, for when he has stood the test he will receive the crown of life, which God has promised to those who love him. 13 Let no one say when he is tempted, "I am being tempted by God," for God cannot be tempted with evil, and he himself tempts no one. 14 But each person is tempted when he is lured and enticed by his own desire. 15 Then desire when it has conceived gives birth to sin, and sin when it is fully grown brings forth death.

16 Do not be deceived, my beloved brothers. 17 Every good gift and every perfect gift is from above, coming down from the Father of lights, with whom there is no variation or shadow due to change.[a] 18 Of his own will he brought us forth by the word of truth, that we should be a kind of firstfruits of his creatures.

_____
_____
_____
_____
_____

Read James 4:1–6:

Warning Against Worldliness
4 What causes quarrels and what causes fights among you? Is it not this, that your passions[a] are at war within you?[b] 2 You desire and do not have, so you murder. You covet and cannot obtain, so you fight and quarrel. You do not have, because you do not ask. 3 You ask and do not receive, because you ask wrongly, to spend it on your passions. 4 You adulterous people![c] Do you not know that friendship with the world is enmity with God? Therefore, whoever wishes to be a friend of the world makes himself an enemy of God. 5 Or do you suppose it is to no purpose that the Scripture says, "He yearns jealously over the spirit that he has made to dwell in us"? 6 But he gives more grace. Therefore, it says, "God opposes the proud but gives grace to the humble.

LESSON 5:
HOW WE LIFE IN THE SPIRIT AND EXPERIENCE GOD'S POWER OVER THE FLESH AND THE ENEMY

___

Read Ephesians 6:13–20:

[13] Therefore take up the whole armor of God, that you may be able to withstand in the evil day, and having done all, to stand firm. [14] Stand therefore, having fastened on the belt of truth, and having put on the breastplate of righteousness, [15] and, as shoes for your feet, having put on the readiness given by the gospel of peace. [16] In all circumstances take up the shield of faith, with which you can extinguish all the flaming darts of the evil one; [17] and take the helmet of salvation, and the sword of the Spirit, which is the word of God, [18] praying at all times in the Spirit, with all prayer and supplication. To that end, keep alert with all perseverance, making supplication for all the saints, [19] and also for me, that words may be given to me in opening my mouth boldly to proclaim the mystery of the gospel, [20] for which I am an ambassador in chains, that I may declare it boldly, as I ought to speak.

___

LESSON 5:
HOW WE LIFE IN THE SPIRIT AND EXPERIENCE GOD'S POWER OVER THE FLESH AND THE ENEMY

Read through these sets of verses and write out the keys to overcoming the life of the flesh (self) and living in the Spirit. What is the role of the Holy Spirit? Why is this so significant to us enjoying life and receiving all that God wants to deliver to us for our Covenant experience in our everyday lives?

Read Matthew 16:24–27:

Take Up Your Cross and Follow Jesus
24 Then Jesus told his disciples, "If anyone would come after me, let him deny himself and take up his cross and follow me. 25 For whoever would save his life[a] will lose it, but whoever loses his life for my sake will find it. 26 For what will it profit a man if he gains the whole world and forfeits his soul? Or what shall a man give in return for his soul? 27 For the Son of Man is going to come with his angels in the glory of his Father, and then he will repay each person according to what he has done.

_____

_____

_____

_____

Read Romans 8:12–17:

Heirs with Christ
12 So then, brothers,[a] we are debtors, not to the flesh, to live according to the flesh. 13 For if you live according to the flesh you will die, but if by the Spirit you put to death the deeds of the body, you will live. 14 For all who are led by the Spirit of God are sons[b] of God. 15 For you did not receive the spirit of slavery to fall back into fear, but you have received the Spirit of adoption as sons, by whom we cry, "Abba! Father!" 16 The Spirit himself bears witness with our spirit that we are children of God, 17 and if children, then heirs—heirs of God and fellow heirs with Christ, provided we suffer with him in order that we may also be glorified with him.

LESSON 5:
HOW WE LIFE IN THE SPIRIT AND EXPERIENCE GOD'S POWER OVER THE FLESH AND THE ENEMY

Read John 16:13–15:

[13] When the Spirit of truth comes, he will guide you into all the truth, for he will not speak on his own authority, but whatever he hears he will speak, and he will declare to you the things that are to come. [14] He will glorify me, for he will take what is mine and declare it to you. [15] All that the Father has is mine; therefore, I said that he will take what is mine and declare it to you.

Read Matthew 18:18–20:

[18] Truly, I say to you, whatever you bind on earth shall be bound in heaven, and whatever you loose on earth shall be loosed[a] in heaven. [19] Again I say to you, if two of you agree on earth about anything they ask, it will be done for them by my Father in heaven. [20] For where two or three are gathered in my name, there am I among them."

LESSON 5:
HOW WE LIFE IN THE SPIRIT AND EXPERIENCE GOD'S POWER OVER THE FLESH AND THE ENEMY

Read through these verses and write out the summary of all the keys to enjoying life in the Spirit. How, then, are we to adjust our lives to walking in the Spirit every day and enjoying the benefits of life in the Spirit?

> **Read Psalm 24:1–10:**
>
> The King of Glory
> A Psalm of David.
> **24** The earth is the Lord's and the fullness thereof,[a]
>   the world and those who dwell therein,
> ² for he has founded it upon the seas
>   and established it upon the rivers.
> ³ Who shall ascend the hill of the Lord?
>   And who shall stand in his holy place?
> ⁴ He who has clean hands and a pure heart,
>   who does not lift up his soul to what is false
>   and does not swear deceitfully.
> ⁵ He will receive blessing from the Lord
>   and righteousness from the God of his salvation.
> ⁶ Such is the generation of those who seek him,
>   who seek the face of the God of Jacob.[b] Selah
> ⁷ Lift up your heads, O gates!
>   And be lifted up, O ancient doors,
>   that the King of glory may come in.
> ⁸ Who is this King of glory?
>   The Lord, strong and mighty,
>   the Lord, mighty in battle!
> ⁹ Lift up your heads, O gates!
>   And lift them up, O ancient doors,
>   that the King of glory may come in.
> ¹⁰ Who is this King of glory?
>   The Lord of hosts,
>   he is the King of glory! Selah

_____
_____
_____
_____
_____

www.ingramcontent.com/pod-product-compliance
Lightning Source LLC
LaVergne TN
LVHW071658060526
838201LV00037B/375